BARBARA BEERY'S

Pink Princess

PARTY COOKBOOK

SIMON & SCHUSTER BOOKS FOR YOUNG READERS
An imprint of Simon & Schuster Children's Publishing Division
1230 Avenue of the Americas, New York, New York 10020
Text copyright © 2011 by Barbara Beery
Photography copyright © 2011 by Zac Williams
Illustrations copyright © 2011 by istockphoto.com/blue67
For information about special discounts for bulk purchases, please contact Simon & Schuster
Special Sales at 1-866-506-1949 or business@simonandschuster.com.
The Simon & Schuster Speakers Bureau can bring authors to your live event.
For more information or to book an event, contact the Simon & Schuster Speakers Bureau
at 1-866-248-3049 or visit our website at www.simonspeakers.com.
Book design by Lucy Ruth Cummins
The text for this book is set in Goudy Old Style.
Manufactured in China
0611 SCP
2 4 6 8 10 9 7 5 3
Library of Congress Cataloging-in-Publication Data
Beery, Barbara, 1954–
Barbara Beery's pink princess party cookbook / Barbara Beery ;
photography by Zac Williams.
p. cm.
ISBN 978-1-4424-1231-6 (hardcover)
1. Entertaining—Juvenile literature. 2. Cookery—Juvenile literature. 3. Children's parties—
Juvenile literature. I. Williams, Zac. II. Title. III. Title: Pink princess party cookbook.
TX731.B385 2011
641.5'123—dc22
2010017691

BARBARA BEERY'S **Pink Princess**

PARTY COOKBOOK

PHOTOGRAPHY BY ZAC WILLIAMS

Simon & Schuster Books for Young Readers
New York London Toronto Sydney

Let's Party!

Anytime is the perfect time to celebrate with a Pink Princess party! These whimsical Princess party themes use all of the recipes in the cookbook. Plan your party using these themes or mix and match the recipes and themes to create your own Pink Princess party spectacular!

Garden Fairy Princess Party

Mermaid Princess Party

Enchanted Pony Princess Party

Pink Princess Party

Notes to Parents
Safety and Age-Appropriate Tasks

★ The recipes in *Pink Princess Party Cookbook* are appropriate for children age 5 and older to make with the assistance of a grown-up.

★ A general guideline for adults helping kids in the kitchen is to allow the child the opportunity to learn one or two tasks or skills at a time.

★ Fit the size of the bowl, utensils, etc. to the size of the child's hand. There are numerous kid-friendly, appropriately sized cooking and baking products available to ensure kids' safety in the kitchen.

★ Children develop hand-to-eye coordination, reading skills, and attention spans at various times within a given age range. Children of different ages will vastly vary in skill levels and their ability to successfully complete a specific hands-on task.

★ Children ages 5 to 7 will need more assistance in reading directions and completing tasks such as prepping items that need knives or take multiple steps to complete.

★ Children age 8 and older will be able to complete many more tasks and recipes in this cookbook on their own with less adult assistance.

★ Encouraging children to make an age-appropriate recipe from start to finish with as much or as little assistance as needed gives them the chance to enjoy a delicious treat as their reward, and allows them to become experts on that particular recipe. Cooking is gratifying, extremely creative, and an ideal activity for all children.

★ If using flowers in your recipes, make sure they are pesticide-free, as seen in the recipe Rose-Berry Punch on page 20.

Welcome to the Pink Princess Kitchen!

Every Pink Princess knows her way around an enchanted kitchen. Here are some simple steps to keep a Princess's kitchen kingdom fun-filled and successful.

Tips, Tricks, and Prep Ideas

★ It's time to get ready for cooking, Pink Princess! Kindly ask a grown-up to be your assistant. Push back your sleeves, tie on a cute little apron, wash your hands, and please make sure your work area is spotless. A clean kitchen is an enchanted kitchen.

★ Read through your recipe with your grown-up assistant. Gather bowls, utensils, gadgets, and all ingredients that will be needed to make the chosen recipe. Place all of these items on your work area (which may be the kitchen table or the kitchen countertop). You may also cover the work area with a piece of foil or use a large cutting board as your work area to keep everything in place.

★ Clean up as you create. The Pink Princess kitchen should always be neat and tidy. Before you begin preparing your recipe, fill a sink with soapy water. Take a sponge or washcloth and a dry kitchen towel to your work area. As you complete each task in the recipe, take all the utensils and bowls and carefully place them in the sink. When your recipe is completed, you'll have almost everything cleaned up!

★ Once more read the recipe with your grown-up assistant. Please make sure that you both understand how the recipe is to be made. You may choose which portion of the recipe that each of you will be responsible to create, or you may simply ask for your grown-up assistant's help when you need it.

★ Read each step of the recipe and take your time. Now you are ready for a royally good time; let's make the recipe!

★ Pink Princess kitchen manners: Please remember to thank your grown-up assistant for helping. A gracious way to thank them is to offer the first bite of your delicious creation. With a reward like that, they'll want to be your assistant every time.

Snowflake PRINCESS PARTY

Snow Princess Punch

1 cup mini marshmallows

½ cup white decorating sugar

½ lemon or orange

One 2-liter bottle fruit-flavored sparkling water, chilled

2 cups frozen blueberries

1. Place mini marshmallows on a cookie sheet. Freeze for 2 hours or until you are ready to add to the punch.

Let's garnish the punch cups!

2. Pour the sugar onto a small plate. Dampen the rim of a large punch bowl and small decorative glasses by rubbing them with a lemon or orange half. Dip the dampened rims into the sugar and set aside until you are ready to serve the punch.

Let's make punch!

3. Pour the sparkling water into the punch bowl. Add the blueberries and marshmallows. Stir. Serve in the garnished punch cups.

A festive frosty punch in a sugar sipper cup

Snow Princess Sandwiches

Makes 12 sandwiches

1 cup soft-spread cream cheese

2 tablespoons mango chutney, chopped

1 cup finely chopped deli turkey

Twelve 10-inch flour tortillas

12 fresh blueberries

2 small star fruits, thinly sliced

Let's make sandwiches!

1. In a mixing bowl, combine the cream cheese, chutney, and chopped turkey. Set aside.

2. Cut out two 3- to 4-inch circles from each tortilla, for a total of 24 tortilla circles. Cover a stack of 12 with a kitchen towel.

3. Heat the remaining 12 tortilla circles in the microwave for 15 to 20 seconds to slightly soften. Keep in the microwave with the door closed. Removing only 1 tortilla at a time, fold each tortilla into quarters and cut into snowflake shapes with a small pair of craft scissors, as if you were making paper snowflakes. Continue until snowflake shapes have been cut into all 12 tortillas.

4. Place equal amounts of filling on the 12 round, uncut tortilla circles. Top each with a snowflake tortilla. Place a blueberry in the center of each sandwich, garnish with star fruit slices, and serve immediately.

May be stored covered in refrigerator for up to 2 hours.

A Snow Princess sandwich tortilla treat

Frosty Donut Ice Cream Treats

Makes 12 treats

2 cups powdered sugar

2 to 3 tablespoons whole milk or half-and-half

½ teaspoon vanilla extract

Pink paste food coloring

12 unfrosted mini cake donuts

½ cup assorted sprinkles or small candies

1 quart vanilla ice cream or raspberry sorbet

Canned whipped topping

Let's make donut treats!

1. Line a cookie sheet with foil or parchment paper and set aside.

2. In a small bowl, combine 2 tablespoons milk or half-and-half and the vanilla. Add the milk mixture, a little at a time, to the powdered sugar. Mix and add the extra tablespoon of milk or half-and-half if necessary to create a smooth icing. Stir in a small amount of pink food coloring, mixing well.

3. Spread the icing on one side of each donut and place on the prepared cookie sheet. Decorate with sprinkles or candies and place the cookie sheet with the iced donuts uncovered in the freezer for at least 1 hour or until you are almost ready to serve.

4. Remove the donuts from the freezer and place 1 scoop of ice cream or sorbet into the hole of each donut. Top with a squirt of whipped topping. Return to the freezer uncovered at least 1 hour, or until you are ready to serve.

May be made up to 8 hours in advance and stored covered after completely frozen.

Tiny donuts and ice cream are every Princess's dream.

5

Snowflake Meringue Cookies

2 large egg whites, room temperature

½ teaspoon cream of tartar

1 cup powdered sugar

1 teaspoon vanilla extract

Colored decorating sugar (optional)

Crispy cookie snowflakes that melt in your mouth

Let's make snowflakes!

1. Preheat the oven to 200 degrees. Line 2 cookie sheets with parchment paper. With a pencil, draw simple 2-inch snowflake shapes with 6 points about ½ inch apart on the parchment paper.

2. In a large, very clean bowl, beat the egg whites and cream of tartar with an electric mixer on medium speed until frothy, about 3 minutes. They will look like soap suds at this point. Turn the mixer speed to high and beat for another 3 minutes or so, until the eggs whites are fluffy like whipped cream.

3. Turn the mixer to low and add the powdered sugar, 2 tablespoons at a time, until all is incorporated into the egg whites. Continue beating until the egg whites are stiff and glossy, about 5 minutes more. Stir in the vanilla extract.

4. Turn the parchment paper sheets pencil side down and stick them to the cookie sheets by dabbing a little meringue in each corner. Spoon the meringue into a large zip-close plastic bag and zip shut. Snip off a tip of one corner with scissors and follow the snowflake tracings on parchment paper, making each snowflake about ½ inch thick. If you like, sprinkle the cookies with colored sugar.

5. Bake the snowflakes until dry but not browned, about 1 hour. Carefully slide the parchment paper from the cookie sheets onto wire racks and let the cookies cool for 1 hour.

6. Carefully remove the snowflakes from the paper and serve immediately.

May be stored covered for up to two weeks.

crystal Candy Necklaces

Makes 1 necklace

1½ yards ¼-inch-wide pastel satin ribbon

3 strands rock candy strings in different pastel colors

A rock candy necklace to wear and to eat

Let's make a necklace!

1. Cut the satin ribbon to the correct length to hang around a child's neck and create a large bow when tied.

2. Cut one color of rock candy into a strand about 3 inches long. Cut the other two colors of candy into 1½- to 2-inch lengths.

3. Tie and double knot the longest strand of rock candy in the center of the ribbon by securing it with a small length of the remaining ribbon. Add the shorter candy strands on either side of the longer strand, attaching them with the remaining pieces of ribbon and making sure to tie and double knot each securely. Cut off any excess ribbon.

4. Place the necklace loosely around the child's neck and tie together the two ends of the ribbon to form a decorative bow at the nape of her neck. This adorable necklace won't last long with that sweet candy hanging from it!

Kid-Friendly Craft Tips

Rock candy strings may be found at traditional candy stores and online specialty candy stores.

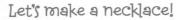

7

Spa PRINCESS PARTY

Spa-Te-Dah Fruit Tea

Serves 10 to 12

1 lemon, thinly sliced

1 orange, thinly sliced

1 cup whole strawberries, with stems removed, not cored

2 kiwis, peeled and thinly sliced

6 mango or peach tea bags

6 cups boiling water

2 cups white grape or white cranberry juice

½ cup honey or agave nectar

Let's make tea!

1. Freeze the lemon, orange, strawberries, and kiwi in a single layer on baking sheets for 1 hour or up to 1 day.

2. In heatproof container, combine the tea and boiling water. Steep for 5 minutes. Remove and discard the tea bags.

3. Stir in the juice and honey or agave nectar with a large spoon Transfer to a container with a lid. Chill for 4 hours or overnight.

4. When you are ready to serve, pour the tea into a punch bowl, add the frozen fruits, stir, and serve.

A pitcher of fruity tea fun for everyone

Enchanted Sushi Roll-Ups

Makes 24 sushi sandwiches

6 slices whole-wheat bread, crusts removed

¼ cup soft-spread cream cheese

3 tablespoons sour cream

1 tablespoon Dijon mustard

1 teaspoon honey

Salt and pepper

Twelve 6-inch-long carrot matchsticks

Twelve 6-inch-long peeled apple matchsticks

3 strawberries, minced

Let's make sushi!

1. Place a sheet of parchment paper on the countertop. With a rolling pin, lightly roll each bread slice on the paper to flatten it.

2. Mix together the cream cheese, sour cream, mustard, honey, and salt and pepper to taste. Spread over each bread slice.

3. Lay 2 carrot matchsticks and 2 apple matchsticks across the bottom of each slice of bread, letting the fruit and veggies hang over the sides. Roll up the bread, pressing gently to seal. With a serrated-edge knife, cut each roll into 4 equal pieces.

4. Garnish with the strawberries and serve.

May be made ahead up to 3 hours in advance.

Enchantingly good, deliciously fun

Chocolate-Dipped Marshmallow Wands

Makes 12 wands

12 large
marshmallows

Twelve 6- to 8-inch
pretzel rods

4 to 6 squares white
candy coating or
white almond bark

Powdered food
coloring in
assorted colors

Assorted
sprinkles and candy
decorations

Let's make marshmallow wands!

1. Insert a craft stick or the end of a butter knife into one end of each marshmallow to create a small opening for the pretzel. Insert a pretzel rod into each marshmallow and place on a foil- or parchment paper–lined cookie sheet.

2. Melt the candy coating or almond bark according to the package directions. Remove from the heat and cool for 5 minutes. Divide the melted candy among several bowls and add a different color of powdered food coloring to each. Stir with a spoon to blend.

3. Dip each marshmallow into a different color of candy coating and decorate with assorted sprinkles and sugars. Place each wand back on the cookie sheet and freeze uncovered for 15 minutes.

4. Cover the wands and store in freezer up to 8 hours.

5. Remove from the freezer and thaw for 5 to 10 minutes before serving.

Watch these
marshmallow
wands magically
disappear.

13

Sparkling Princess Body Lotion

Makes 1 cup lotion

½ cup lotion or body cream

½ cup aloe vera gel

1 tablespoon colored craft glitter

4 to 5 drops fruit- or flower-scented fragrant oils, or a combination of both

Let's make lotion!

Combine all the ingredients in a small mixing bowl with whisk. Place in a clean jar with lid. To use, smooth onto arms and legs. Store up to 2 weeks.

A sweet-scented, sparkling lotion potion

Terry Cloth Flip-Flops

Makes 1 pair flip-flops

1 pair flip-flops

¼ yard pink terry cloth

Tacky glue

Assorted silk flowers, decorative buttons, bows, or scrapbook materials

Little Princess tootsies will wiggle with glee.

Let's decorate flip-flops!

1. Carefully disassemble each flip-flop by taking the toe portion completely out of the shoe.

2. Lay the flip-flops on top of the terry cloth and trace the outline of the shoe. Cut out the traced pieces of fabric. Place each piece on a flip-flop and mark where the holes for the toe portion will be. Cut a hole on each piece of fabric with a hole punch or snip a small hole with scissors.

3. Glue the pieces of fabric to each flip-flop with tacky glue. Let sit for 10 minutes to dry.

4. Carefully slip the toe portion back in the hole of each flip-flop.

5. Fold the remaining fabric in half. Cut 2 long lengthwise strips, ½-inch wide. Glue one end of the 1 fabric strip to the toe portion of the strap and wrap it around to completely cover one strap. Cut off any extra fabric. Secure the end to the flip-flop with glue. Cover the other strap of the flip-flop with the other fabric strip and cut and secure in the same way.

6. Attach a flower, button, or other decoration to the top center of each flip-flop strap and glue to secure. Allow the glue to dry for 1 hour before wearing.

Kid-Friendly Craft Tips

Tacky glue may be found in craft stores and is child friendly and kid safe. It dries quickly, dries clear, and adheres wonderfully to all fabrics and textures.

Ribbons and Bows Flip-Flops

Makes 1 pair flip-flops

2 yards ¼- to ½-inch-wide solid, striped, or patterned grosgrain ribbon

1 pair flip-flops

Tacky glue

Purchased curly ribbon gift bows, 1½ to 2 inches in diameter

2 buttons, rhinestones, or large sparkly beads

Let's decorate flip-flops!

1. Cut the ribbon in half. Start with one flip-flop. Using one piece of ribbon for each flip-flop strap, wrap each side with the ribbon, cut to fit, and secure both ends with tacky glue.

2. Tie the curly ribbon bow onto the center top section of the flip-flop where the two straps join. Secure with tacky glue.

3. Decorate the center of the bow with a colorful button, rhinestone, or large sparkly bead.

4. Repeat the same procedure on the other flip-flop.

5. Allow the glue to dry for 1 hour before wearing.

Kid-Friendly Craft Tips

Craft and fabric stores provide a multitude of options for decorating flip-flops. Yarn, tulle, or satin ribbon may be substituted for grosgrain ribbon.

Scrapbook supply stores have all sorts of decorative finishes to create your very own personalized pair of flip-flops!

17

Garden Fairy PRINCESS PARTY

Rose-Berry Punch

Serves 10 to 12

2 quarts cranberry-apple-raspberry juice cocktail, chilled

One 2-liter bottle unflavored sparkling water, chilled

½ cup rose petal syrup or grenadine syrup

2 pints fresh raspberries, strawberries, or blackberries

Edible pesticide-free assorted whole flowers and pink rose petals

Let's make punch!

1. Pour the juice and sparkling water into a large punch bowl.

2. Slowly stir in the syrup, tasting regularly until you reach the sweetness and fragrance you want.

3. Carefully stir in ice cubes and the berries. Float the flowers on top and ladle the punch into cups. Top each cup of punch with a few rose petals.

Kid-Friendly Tips and Tricks

Rose petal syrup may be found in the international foods section of some supermarkets. Grenadine syrup is readily available in all supermarkets and may be substituted for the rose petal syrup but will not add a rose scent or taste to the punch.

Try making homemade rose petal syrup—it's easy! Place 6 cups water, 2 cups sugar, and 2 cups pesticide-free rose petals in a large saucepan. Stir. Bring to boil for 10 minutes, remove from the heat, cool, strain, and store in a covered storage container in the refrigerator for up to 2 weeks.

Fruit and flowers give a Princess magic powers.

Wildflower Quiche Cups

Nonstick cooking spray

All-purpose flour

One 17.3-ounce package refrigerated pie crust

2 large eggs

½ cup chopped yellow bell pepper

¼ teaspoon table salt

⅛ teaspoon ground pepper

½ cup heavy cream or half-and-half

½ cup grated Swiss or Gruyère cheese

Pitted black olives, halved crosswise

1 green bell pepper, cut into thin strips and leaf shapes

Let's make quiche!

1. Preheat the oven to 400 degrees. Generously spray the 12 cups of a muffin pan with cooking spray.

2. Flatten the pie crusts and dust them with the flour. Cut out 12 shapes with a 2- to 3-inch flower-shaped cookie cutter. Place a cutout in each muffin-pan cup. (Rewrap and freeze any leftover pie crust for another use.)

3. Prick the bottom of each crust with the tines of a fork. Set aside.

4. In a medium bowl, use a whisk to combine the eggs, yellow bell pepper, salt, pepper, cream, and cheese. Pour the mixture into the pastry shells, filling each one almost to the top.

5. Bake for 10 to 15 minutes, until slightly puffed and lightly browned.

6. Remove from the oven and cool for 5 minutes in the muffin pan on a wire rack. Transfer the quiches from the muffin pan to the wire rack and press half an olive into the center of each to create the center of the flower.

7. To serve, put 1 quiche on each plate and use the green pepper to create a stem and leaves.

A little flower quiche that's almost too cute to eat

21

Fairytale Flowerpot Dessert

Makes 12 desserts

1 fresh pineapple, cut into 12 round slices

Seedless red and green grapes, raspberries and blackberries

Twelve 6-inch wooden skewers

Twelve new 2-inch clay flowerpots and saucers, washed and dried

1 purchased, 16-ounce angel food or pound cake, cut into 2-inch cubes

1 quart ice cream or your favorite frozen confection, any flavor

¾ to 1 cup chocolate syrup

Assorted sprinkles

12 colorful straws cut to fit the length of the skewers

A fancy, fruity ice cream dessert

Let's make flowerpot desserts!

1. Line 2 cookie sheets with foil or parchment paper and set aside.

2. To make fruit flowers, cut out the center of each pineapple slice with a small melon baller. Cut each slice into a flower shape with a 2- to 3-inch flower-shaped metal cookie cutter. Place a grape, raspberry, or blackberry in the cut-out center of the pineapple flower.

3. Insert a wooden skewer starting at the bottom of the pineapple flower, carefully pushing it through the fruit in the center and through the top portion of the pineapple flower, making sure the skewer is not sticking out the top of the flower. Place the flowers on a cookie sheet in the refrigerator.

4. Place the flowerpots in their saucers and set on the other cookie sheet. Put several cubes of cake into each pot, filling it halfway to the top. Press down on the cake, making sure to cover the hole in the bottom of each pot. Fill each flowerpot with a scoop of ice cream. Drizzle with chocolate syrup and garnish with sprinkles.

5. Insert a straw into the center of the ice cream. Store the flowerpots in the freezer until you are ready to serve.

6. When you are ready to serve, remove the flowerpots from the freezer and the fruit flowers from the refrigerator. Insert a flower into the straw in each flowerpot and serve immediately.

May be stored covered up to 8 hours.

23

Pretty Pink Ladybug Cupcakes

Makes 24 cupcakes

Cupcakes

1 box yellow cake mix

Eggs or egg whites and butter or oil, the amounts called for on the cake mix package

Green paste food coloring

1 teaspoon vanilla extract

½ teaspoon almond extract

Frosting and Decorations

1 tub vanilla frosting

Pink paste food coloring

White cookie icing

48 small sugar candy eyes

24 fudge-covered Oreos

Red cookie icing

Cherry or Twizted Berry Twizzlers, separated to make 12 to 15 individual strands

1 large bag M&M's Chocolate Mini Baking Bits, brown ones only

Let's make cupcakes!

1. Preheat the oven to 350 degrees. Line 24 muffin-pan cups with bright green paper cupcake liners.

2. Make and bake the cupcakes according to the package directions, adding 10 drops of green food coloring and the vanilla and almond extracts to the other wet ingredients.

3. Remove the cupcakes from the oven and cool on wire racks for 15 minutes. Put the cupcakes on cookie sheets and place in the freezer for 30 minutes.

4. Combine the vanilla frosting and 5 drops of pink food coloring in a mixing bowl. Remove the cupcakes from the freezer and frost with the pink frosting.

5. With a small amount of white cookie icing, glue 2 candy eyes on each fudge-covered Oreo. Draw a thin curved line with the red cookie icing to create a mouth on each Oreo. Place the decorated Oreo on the upper edge of the cupcake to create the ladybug's head. Cut the separated Twizzler strands into short lengths to form the ladybug's lines on her back (for wings). Arrange M&M's on the frosting to create ladybug spots.

6. Serve immediately.

Cupcakes can be stored covered up to 3 days prior to frosting and decorating. Once frosted, store cupcakes uncovered for up to 3 hours.

A ladybug cupcake treat that a Princess can make and eat

24

Jeweled Flower Headbands

Makes 1 headband

Buttons, rhinestones, and beads in assorted sizes and colors

Silk flowers, scrapbook flowers, or 1 to 2 yards of colorful felt fabric to cut out flower shapes

Tacky glue

One 1½- to 2-inch-wide knit headband

Let's decorate headbands!

1. Create decorative flowers by attaching buttons, rhinestones, and beads to the silk, scrapbook, or felt flowers with glue.

2. Attach the decorative flowers to the headband with more glue.

3. Allow the glue to dry for 1 hour before wearing the headband.

The floral-crowned jewel of all headbands

Enchanted Pony PRINCESS PARTY

Pink Pony Pink Hot Chocolate

Serves 10 to 12

10 to 12 large marshmallows

1 teaspoon cornstarch

2 quarts vanilla soy milk (regular or light)

2 cups white chocolate chips (one 12-ounce bag)

2 teaspoons vanilla extract

¼ cup grenadine syrup or maraschino cherry juice

Pink sprinkles

Let's make hot chocolate!

1. Place the marshmallows and cornstarch in a large zip-close plastic bag. Shake to coat the marshmallows. (This will keep them from sticking to the mini cookie cutters.)

2. Remove the marshmallows from the bag and press each one with your hand to flatten it. Use a 1-inch (or smaller) cookie cutter to cut the marshmallows into assorted shapes. Set aside.

3. Heat the milk in a saucepan over low heat until simmering. Add the white chocolate chips and stir constantly with a whisk until they have melted and combined with the milk. Remove from the heat and stir in the vanilla extract and grenadine syrup or maraschino cherry juice. Garnish with the marshmallows and pink sprinkles and serve immediately.

Hot chocolate may be covered and stored at room temperature for up to hours. Reheat over low heat, garnish, and serve.

A prancing pony's favorite pink drink

Ponytail Pasta K-Bobs

Makes 12 k-bobs

One 9-ounce package
cheese tortellini

Twelve 6-inch
wooden skewers

1 small bunch each
seedless red and
green grapes

12 or more edible,
pesticide-free flowers,
for garnish

Let's make pasta k-bobs!

1. Line a cookie sheet with foil.

2. Cook the tortellini according to the package directions. Drain, rinse, and let cool slightly.

3. Carefully place the tortellini and grapes on each skewer, alternating tortellini and grapes.

4. Secure a flower through the stem end of each k-bob and place the completed k-bobs on the serving tray. Serve immediately.

May be covered and stored on a cookie sheet in the refrigerator for up to 3 hours. Remove and let stand at room temperature 1 hour before serving.

Pasta on a stick
is a clever Princess
cooking trick.

Candy Land Ice Cream Cones

Nonstick cooking spray

One 14-ounce package pink candy coating

12 flat-bottomed ice cream cones

1 quart vanilla ice cream, or your favorite frozen confection

Canned whipped topping

Assorted sprinkles

12 small lollipops

Let's make ice cream cones!

1. Spray the inside of 12 muffin-pan cups with cooking spray. Set aside.

2. Melt the candy coating according to the package directions and pour into a mixing bowl.

3. Holding the cones one at a time upside down over the bowl, spoon candy coating over each. Place the coated cones upside down in the muffin pans. Freeze uncovered for 15 minutes to harden the candy coating.

4. Remove from the freezer and fill each cone with ice cream. Garnish with a squirt of whipped topping and some sprinkles. Insert a lollipop into the center of each ice cream cone and serve.

To prepare in advance, coat and chill the cones, fill with ice cream, and place in the freezer until serving time (no longer than 8 hours). When you are ready to serve, remove them from the freezer and garnish with the whipped topping, sprinkles, and lollipops.

Ice cream cones drizzled with melted candy are dandy.

Prancing Pony cupcakes

CUPCAKES

1 package strawberry cake mix

Eggs and oil, the amounts called for on the cake mix package

1 teaspoon vanilla extract

½ teaspoon almond extract

BUTTERCREAM FROSTING

4 cups powdered sugar, more if needed

Pinch of salt

¼ to ½ cup half-and-half or whole milk

8 tablespoons (1 stick) unsalted butter, room temperature

Paste food coloring in assorted colors

COOKIES

1 tub vanilla frosting

1 teaspoon meringue powder

Paste food colorings in assorted colors

24 I'm a Little Princess Cookies (page 50), cut out with a small pony cookie cutter

Assorted sprinkles

Let's make cupcakes!

1. Preheat oven to 350 degrees. Line 24 muffin-pan cups with paper cupcake liners or place 24 silicone muffin cups on 2 cookie sheets.

2. Make and bake cupcakes according to the package directions, adding the strawberry and almond extracts to the other wet ingredients. Remove from the oven and cool the cupcakes in the pans on wire racks for 5 minutes. Remove the cupcakes from the pans and cool for another 15 minutes on wire racks.

3. Place the cooled cupcakes uncovered on cookie sheets in the freezer for 15 minutes before frosting and decorating.

You could also freeze the cupcakes 15 minutes, then cover them and store for up to 1 week before frosting and decorating.

Let's make buttercream frosting!

4. Place the powdered sugar and salt in a large bowl and mix with a whisk to break up lumps.

5. Add ¼ cup of the half-and-half to the powdered sugar and mix with an electric mixer on low speed. Add the butter, turn the mixer up to high, and beat until fluffy. You may need to add a little more liquid if the mixture is too thick or a little more powdered sugar if the mixture is too thin. With the mixer on low, beat in the vanilla.

6. Divide the frosting into several small bowls and beat a different color into each one. Cover the bowls.

Let's make pony cookies!

7. Combine the vanilla frosting and meringue powder. Divide the frosting into several bowls and beat a different color into each one. Frost each pony cookie and decorate with sprinkles. Let the cookies dry for 30 minutes uncovered.

You could also let each decorated cookie dry for 15 minutes, then carefully cover and store up to 1 day before using on the cupcakes.

8. When you are ready to decorate them, remove the cupcakes from the freezer and frost with the buttercream frosting. Insert a decorated pony cookie into the center of each cupcake. Serve immediately.

Store the frosted cupcakes uncovered at room temperature without inserting the decorated pony cookies for up to 3 hours before serving. Add the cookies and serve.

A carousel of colorful cupcakes for a Pony Princess

Fluffy Puffy Pony Crowns

Makes 1 crown

One ½-inch-wide plastic headband

1 yard pastel grosgrain ribbon, 1¼ to 1½ inches wide

Tacky glue

1 roll each pink, purple, and white tulle ribbon, 3 to 4 inches wide

Let's make a crown!

1. Cover the headband with grosgrain ribbon, trim, and attach each end with glue.

2. Cut tulle into seven or eight 6- to 7-inch strips. Cut one other strip of tulle approximately 18 inches long.

3. Tie the shorter strips into double knots at regular intervals on the headband. Cut each knotted tulle strip to about 3 inches in length and fluff out.

4. Tie the 18-inch length of tulle in a double knot to form a veil or ponytail in the center of the headband.

5. Allow the glue to dry for 1 hour before wearing the crown.

Kid-Friendly Craft Tips

Tulle by the roll is the suggested material choice, but tulle may also be purchased by the yard and cut into the appropriate width needed. Just ¼ to ½ yard of each color of tulle will be ample to make 1 headband.

This beautiful crown will make every Princess the toast of the town.

Mermaid Castle Party Punch

Serves 10 to 12

One .22-ounce package unsweetened Berry Blue Kool-Aid Twists

1 cup sugar

1 quart pineapple-coconut juice, chilled

One 2-liter bottle lemon-lime soda, chilled

1 quart vanilla ice cream, thawed until pourable

Oceans of sweet, fruity foam in every glass

Let's make punch!

Pour the Kool-Aid and sugar into a punch bowl. Stir in the pineapple-coconut juice with a whisk. Add the lemon-lime soda. Stir in the ice cream and serve immediately.

The punch may be covered and stored in the refrigerator up to 8 hours before adding the soda and ice cream. To serve, remove from the refrigerator and add the soda and ice cream. Stir well and serve.

Tea-by-the-sea sandwiches

Makes 12 sandwiches

¼ cup mayonnaise

1 teaspoon Dijon mustard

3 tablespoons prepared basil pesto

One 5-ounce can water-packed solid white tuna, drained

1 large celery rib, diced

½ small red bell pepper, diced

24 slices whole-wheat bread, cut into assorted sea-themed shapes

Red, green, or yellow bell pepper pieces, for garnish

Let's make sandwiches!

1. Place mayonnaise, mustard, and pesto in a medium bowl. Whisk to blend.

2. Add the tuna, celery, and red bell pepper. Toss the ingredients together with a fork to coat thoroughly.

3. Spread equal amounts of the tuna salad on the tops of 12 cut-out pieces of bread. Place another slice of the same shape on top of that. Gently press to hold together.

4. Cut tiny circles of red, green, or yellow bell peppers to make eyes for the sea animals and place them on top of the sandwiches. Serve immediately.

Magic Wand Starfish Cookies

Makes 12 to 15 cookies

12 tablespoons (1½ stick) unsalted butter, room temperature

½ cup light brown sugar, packed

1 large egg

¾ cup molasses

3 cups all-purpose flour

¼ teaspoon table salt

2 teaspoons ground ginger

1 teaspoon ground cinnamon

½ teaspoon ground cloves

½ teaspoon ground nutmeg

Nonstick cooking spray

Powdered sugar

Assorted candy sticks or craft sticks

Small and large star-shaped candies

½ cup turbinado sugar or Sugar in the Raw

Assorted ribbons

Let's make starfish cookies!

1. In a large mixing bowl, combine the butter, brown sugar, egg, and molasses with an electric mixer on medium speed.

2. Stir in the flour, salt, ginger, cinnamon, cloves, and nutmeg. Mix completely. Place the cookie dough in a large zip-close plastic bag and refrigerate overnight.

3. Preheat the oven to 350 degrees. Line 2 cookie sheets with foil or parchment paper. Lightly spray with cooking spray. Dust a large piece of parchment paper with powdered sugar.

4. Take out one quarter of the dough from the refrigerator, leaving the rest of the dough in the bag in the refrigerator until you need it. Roll out the dough to ½-inch thick on the parchment paper. With a 2- to 3-inch star-shaped cookie cutter, cut out the dough. Reroll and recut the rest of the chilled cookie dough until all is used.

5. Place the cookie cutouts on the cookie sheets, 2 inches apart. Press a candy or craft stick between two star points in each cookie. Use a little extra cookie dough to cover most of the stick.

6. Curve each star point with your fingers to resemble a starfish. Decorate each cookie with a small star candy on each point and a larger star in the center.

7. Bake for 8 to 12 minutes, until light golden brown.

8. Remove the cookies from the oven and immediately sprinkle generously with turbinado sugar while warm. Cool on the cookie sheets for 5 minutes before transferring to wire racks to cool for 15 minutes longer.

9. Tie ribbons and bows onto each starfish wand and serve immediately.

May be stored in a covered container for up to 8 hours.

40

Twinkle,
twinkle,
little
starfish
wand

Tropical Island Pudding Pops

One 3.4-ounce package instant vanilla pudding mix

Reduced-fat milk, the amount called for on the pudding package

1 cup frozen whipped topping, thawed

1 teaspoon vanilla extract

¼ teaspoon coconut extract

¼ teaspoon strawberry extract

Food coloring (gel or paste) in lime green, bright pink, and turquoise

Decorating sugars in assorted colors

A frozen tropical treat for a cool Princess to eat

Let's make pudding pops!

1. Make the pudding according to the package directions. Stir in the whipped topping and the vanilla, coconut, and strawberry extracts.

2. Divide the pudding into 3 small bowls. To one bowl, add a small amount of lime green food coloring; to the second bowl, add a small amount of bright pink food coloring; and to the third bowl, add a small amount of turquoise food coloring. Stir each bowl with a separate spoon or clean whisk to blend the color.

3. Fill each pop mold to within ½ inch of the top. Freeze for 4 to 6 hours or overnight.

4. To serve, remove each pop from the mold by holding your hand around the mold to warm it slightly, or run tepid water over the mold, being careful not to get water inside. Lay pops on a cookie sheet. Brush each with a little water. Sprinkle one side of each generously with decorating sugar.

5. Cover with foil and freeze until ready to use, or serve immediately.

Rainbow Fish Face Paints

Makes 2 cups face paint

½ cup cold cream
1 cup cornstarch
½ cup water
Paste food colorings in assorted colors

Princesses, grab your paintbrushes and let the face painting begin.

Let's make face paints!

1. With a whisk, mix the cold cream and cornstarch together in a bowl until blended. Whisk in the water, a little at a time, until smooth and creamy.

2. Divide into several small bowls and add a different color of food coloring to each. Whisk to blend each color completely. Pour into individual containers with lids to store up to 2 weeks.

Pink Princess Lemonade

Serves 10 to 12

Fruit Ice Cubes
24 maraschino cherries

6 thin slices lemon, cut in quarters

1 liter distilled or filtered water

Lemonade
One 2-liter bottle strawberry-flavored sparkling water, chilled

½ cup grenadine syrup

Juice of 8 to 10 lemons (about 1 cup)

1 cup sugar, more or less to taste

Let's make fruit ice cubes!

1. Place 1 cherry and ¼ of a lemon slice in each of 24 ice cube tray sections. Carefully pour distilled water equally into each section, until about ¾ full. Freeze at least 4 hours, until cubes are frozen solid.

Let's make lemonade!

2. In a punch bowl, combine the sparkling water, grenadine syrup, lemon juice, and sugar. Stir well with a whisk to blend.

3. Remove the ice cubes from the freezer and add to the punch bowl. Serve immediately.

Kid-Friendly Tips and Tricks

To show off pretty fruits in ice cubes for a party punch, use distilled or filtered water to make crystal clear ice cubes.

The perfect punch for a Pink Princess party

Princess Tiara Pizzas

Makes 12 pizzas

Nonstick cooking
spray

12 whole-wheat
7-inch tortillas

12 slices mozzarella
cheese, cut into
crowns

1 yellow bell pepper,
seeded, and sliced
into 2-inch strips

1 red bell pepper,
seeded, and sliced
into 2-inch strips

1 green bell pepper,
seeded, and sliced
into 2-inch strips

Let's make pizzas!

1. Preheat the oven to 350 degrees. Line a cookie sheet with foil and lightly spray with cooking spray.

2. Using several geometrically shaped 1-inch pastry cutters, cut the peppers into assorted shapes.

3. Warm 2 to 3 tortillas at a time in the microwave for 30 seconds to soften and make them easier to cut. With a 3- to 4-inch crown-shaped cookie cutter, cut 1 crown from each warmed tortilla. Place the cut-out tortilla crowns on the cookie sheet. Continue until all tortillas have been cut into crown shapes.

4. Place the cheese cutouts on top of the tortilla cutouts and garnish with the 3 assorted colors and shapes of bell peppers.

5. Bake the pizza crowns for 7 to 10 minutes, until cheese is slightly melted. Remove from the oven and cool on the cookie sheet for 5 minutes. Serve immediately.

The only shaped
pizza that a
Princess shall eat

Pink Princess Crown Cake

CAKE

Nonstick cooking spray

8 tablespoons (1 stick) unsalted butter, room temperature

1 cup sugar

2 large eggs

2 teaspoons vanilla extract

1 teaspoon strawberry extract

Pink paste food coloring

2 teaspoons baking powder

¼ teaspoon table salt

1½ cups all-purpose flour

½ cup milk

BUTTERCREAM FROSTING

4 tablespoons (½ stick) unsalted butter, room temperature

4 cups powdered sugar

2 tablespoons milk or half-and-half, more if the frosting is too stiff to spread

1 teaspoon vanilla extract

Pink paste food coloring

Assorted candies and sprinkles

A perfectly royal cake for every Pink Princess

Let's make a Princess cake!

1. Preheat the oven to 350 degrees. Spray the inside of one 8-inch round cake pan and one 6-inch round cake pan with cooking spray. Line the bottom of each pan with a circle of waxed paper or parchment paper.

2. In a medium bowl, cream together the butter and sugar with an electric mixer at medium speed. Beat in the eggs, one at a time. Stir in the vanilla and strawberry extracts and a dab of food coloring for color.

3. In another bowl, stir the baking powder, salt, and flour together with a whisk. Add to the butter mixture alternately with the milk. Beat at medium speed until smooth and creamy, about 1 minute.

4. Pour the batter into the cake pans.

5. Bake for 30 to 35 minutes. The smaller layer may be done a few minutes before the bigger one. The layers should be golden brown. When you touch the top lightly, you should not leave a fingerprint.

6. Cool the layers in the pans for 10 to 15 minutes. Carefully remove them by placing a plate or rack over each pan and inverting the layer onto the plate or rack. Cool another 10 to 15 minutes before frosting.

Let's make frosting!

7. Beat the butter with an electric mixer in a large bowl until butter is soft and fluffy. Slowly add the powdered sugar, ½ cup at a time, alternately with the milk. Beat in the vanilla.

8. Beat in a tiny bit of pink food coloring. Add extra milk, 1 teaspoon at a time, if necessary.

9. When the layers are cool, center the smaller layer on top of the larger one.

10. Frost the cake and decorate with candies and sprinkles.

I'm a Little Princess Cookie

Makes 12 to 15 cookies

Nonstick cooking spray

8 tablespoons (1 stick) unsalted butter, room temperature

¾ cup granulated sugar

1 large egg

1 teaspoon vanilla extract

Pink paste food coloring

2 cups all-purpose flour

½ teaspoon baking soda

¼ teaspoon table salt

Powdered sugar

12 to 15 candy sticks or craft sticks

Cookie or decorator icing

Small candy stars, rounds, and hearts

Edible markers

12 to 15 small candy crowns

Let's make Princess cookies!

1. Preheat the oven to 375 degrees. Line 2 cookie sheets with foil or parchment paper. Spray lightly with cooking spray and set aside.

2. Cream butter with an electric mixer in a large bowl. Add the sugar, beating until light and fluffy. Add the egg, vanilla, and a tiny bit of pink food coloring and mix well at medium speed.

3. Add the flour, baking soda, and salt. Blend well. The dough will be very stiff.

4. Roll out the dough on parchment paper that has been lightly dusted with powdered sugar. Roll the dough until it's ¼- to ½-inch thick. Cut out hearts with a 2-inch heart-shaped cookie cutter. Place the cookies 2 inches apart on the cookie sheets.

5. Press a candy stick into each cookie at the pointed end of the heart. Use a little extra cookie dough to cover most of the stick. Flatten the extra dough slightly.

6. Bake for 8 to 10 minutes, until lightly browned.

7. Remove the cookies from the oven and cool on the cookie sheets for 5 minutes. Transfer the cookies to wire racks to completely cool for another 15 minutes before frosting and decorating.

Let's decorate Princess cookies!

8. Turn each cookie over so that you will be decorating the flat side of the cookie. With a dab of decorator or cookie icing, attach star-shaped candies as eyes and round candies and heart candies as noses and mouths.

9. Draw eyelashes around the eyes with edible markers. Create some round, rosy cheeks, and extend lines on each side of the heart mouth to create a happy smile.

10. Draw hair around the top and sides of each cookie with the cookie or decorator icing and garnish with a small candy crown. Serve immediately.

Kid-Friendly Tips and Tricks

Use powdered sugar instead of flour when you roll out cookie dough. Too much flour in cookie dough toughens the baked cookie.

Edible markers may be found at craft or cake supply stores.

A cookie
Princess
reigns
supreme.

May be stored uncovered in the
refrigerator for up to 8 hours. Remove
from the refrigerator 30 minutes before
serving.

Pink Princess Tiaras

About 70 beads in assorted sizes and colors

3 white, pink, or purple pipe cleaners

1 plastic headband, approximately ¼ inch wide

Assorted larger jewels for decorating

Tacky glue

Let's make tiaras!

1. Thread the beads onto the pipe cleaners.

2. Wrap one end of the first beaded pipe cleaner around the headband and twist to secure. Apply a small amount of glue to secure the pipe cleaner to the headband.

3. Space the beads out evenly and continue to wrap the pipe cleaners around the headband until beads are evenly dispersed and three arches have been created, with the arch in the center of the tiara the highest. (See photograph for example of how it will look.)

4. To hide the pipe cleaners in the front of the tiara and to enhance the overall appearance, glue jewels to the front of the headband. Allow the glue to dry for 1 hour before wearing the tiara.

A beautiful handmade tiara to adorn a Princess

52

INDEX

Metric Conversions
LIQUID AND DRY MEASURES

U.S.	Canadian	Australian
¼ teaspoon	1 mL	1 ml
½ teaspoon	2.5 mL	2.5 ml
1 teaspoon	5 mL	5 ml
1 tablespoon	15 mL	15 ml
¼ cup	60 mL	60 ml
⅓ cup	80 mL	80 ml
½ cup	125 mL	125 ml
⅔ cup	160 mL	160 ml
¾ cup	180 mL	180 ml
1 cup	250 mL	250 ml
1 quart	1 litre	1 litre

TEMPERATURES

Fahrenheit	Celsius
250°	120°
275°	135°
300°	150°
325°	160°
350°	180°
375°	190°
400°	200°
425°	220°
450°	230°
475°	240°
500°	250°